MW01226455

Not Only Journals VIP Club

Join our VIP Club where we'll notify you anytime there is a special offer. Visit the link below, put your email in the box and you will be the first to know of our new releases, freebies, discounts and giveaways.

http://NotOnlyJournals.com/VIPaccess/

20890124R00064

Made in the USA
San Bernardino, CA
30 December 2018